SUPER
SIMPLE
ORIGAMI

ORIGAMI PETS

Easy & Fun Paper-Folding Projects

Anna George

Consulting Editor, Diane Craig, M.A./Reading Specialist

Super Sandcastle

An Imprint of Abdo Publishing
abdopublishing.com

abdopublishing.com

Published by Abdo Publishing, a division of ABDO, PO Box 398166, Minneapolis, Minnesota 55439.
Copyright © 2017 by Abdo Consulting Group, Inc. International copyrights reserved in all countries.
No part of this book may be reproduced in any form without written permission from the publisher.
Super SandCastle™ is a trademark and logo of Abdo Publishing.

Printed in the United States of America, North Mankato, Minnesota
102016
012017

THIS BOOK CONTAINS
RECYCLED MATERIALS

Editor: Liz Salzmann
Content Developer: Nancy Tuminelly
Cover and Interior Design and Production: Mighty Media, Inc.
Photo Credits: iStockphoto; Mighty Media, Inc.
Special Thanks to Kazuko Collins

The following manufacturers/names appearing in this book are trademarks: Elmer's® Glue-All®

Publisher's Cataloging-in-Publication Data
Names: George, Anna, author.
Title: Origami pets: easy & fun paper-folding projects / by Anna George.
Other titles: Easy & fun paper-folding projects | Easy and fun paper-folding projects
Description: Minneapolis, MN : Abdo Publishing, 2017. | Series: Super simple origami
Identifiers: LCCN 2016944712 | ISBN 9781680784503 (lib. bdg.) |
    ISBN 9781680798036 (ebook)
Subjects: LCSH: Animals in art--Juvenile literature. | Origami--Juvenile literature.
    Paper work--Juvenile literature. | Handicraft--Juvenile literature.
Classification: DDC 736/.982--dc23
LC record available at http://lccn.loc.gov/2016944712

Super SandCastle™ books are created by a team of professional educators, reading specialists, and content developers around five essential components—phonemic awareness, phonics, vocabulary, text comprehension, and fluency—to assist young readers as they develop reading skills and strategies and increase their general knowledge. All books are written, reviewed, and leveled for guided reading and early reading intervention programs for use in shared, guided, and independent reading and writing activities to support a balanced approach to literacy instruction.

CONTENTS

AMAZING ORIGAMI
PETS

Origami is the art of folding paper. In Japanese, the word *ori* means "to fold" and *gami* means "paper." People in Japan and all around the world enjoy origami.

Do you have a favorite pet? Is it a dog? Or maybe a rabbit? This book will show you how to make those animals and more! These super simple origami projects are great for beginners. You will learn about:

> ▶ different types of paper folds
> ▶ **symbols** used in origami **diagrams**
> ▶ types of paper that will work for origami

You'll be **amazed** at what you can make with just one sheet of paper!

BASIC FOLDS

MOUNTAIN FOLD
Fold behind to create a mountain.

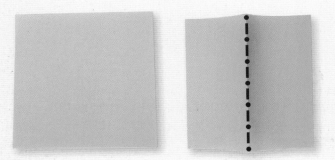

VALLEY FOLD
Fold in front to create a valley.

CREASE
Fold and unfold to make a **crease**.

ORIGAMI SYMBOLS

The **symbols** below show the most common actions used in origami.

– – – – – – – – – –	Valley fold
–·–·–·–·–·–·–	Mountain fold
———————	**Crease**
⟵⟶	Fold and unfold
⟶	Fold toward the front side
⟶	Fold toward the back side
⟿	Turn over
↻	Rotate
⟶	Pull or push
———————	Cut with scissors

SPECIAL FOLDS

INSIDE REVERSE FOLD

This fold is often used to make the head or feet of an animal.
It may seem hard at first. After you practice it will become easier.
Here are instructions to make this fold.

1

Fold a square piece of
paper into a triangle. Valley
fold one of the points.

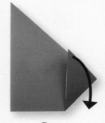

2

Crease it firmly.
Unfold.

3

Mountain fold the
crease. Unfold.

4

Unfold the paper. Place it so the
center crease is vertical. Valley
fold the bottom point.

5

Refold the
center crease.

OUTSIDE REVERSE FOLD

This fold is often used to make the head of a bird or the feet of an animal. It is just like the inside **reverse** fold except the corner is folded on the outside.

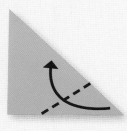

1

Fold a square piece of paper into a triangle. Valley fold one of the points.

2

Crease it firmly. Unfold.

3

Mountain fold the crease. Unfold.

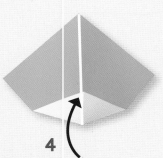

4

Unfold the paper and turn it over. Place it so the center crease is vertical. Valley fold the bottom point.

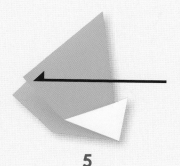

5

Refold the center crease.

MATERIALS

BONE FOLDER

CRAFT STICK

PAPER

You can use almost any type of paper for origami. You can get special origami paper at craft stores or online. You can also use copy paper, magazine pages, scrapbooking paper, and even gift wrap!

CREASING TOOLS

The edge of a ruler, craft stick, or bone folder can help you make good **creases** and folds.

SCISSORS

You will need scissors if you are starting with a sheet of paper that isn't square. (See page 13.)

EXTRAS

These are **optional** supplies used in this book.

- googly eyes
- glue
- markers

TIPS AND TRICKS

GET SQUARE

Many origami models use a square piece of paper.
It is easy to make a rectangular piece of paper square.

1 Fold one short edge so it lines up with a long edge.
Crease the fold.

2 Cut off the strip under the triangle.

3 Unfold the paper. Now you have a square!

PRACTICE MAKES PERFECT!

When folding origami models, it is important for the folds to
be as **accurate** as possible. Match up the edges and corners
when folding. Make firm creases. The more folds there are,
the more important it is to make them exact. So get out some
scrap paper and practice, practice, practice!

RESTING BUNNY

- paper (square)
- scissors
- googly eyes
- glue

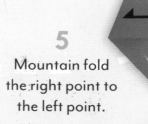

1

Place the paper on the table with one point at the top. Your bunny will be the color of the facedown side.

2

Valley fold the right point to the left point. Unfold.

3

Valley fold the side points to the center **crease**.

4

Turn the model over from top to bottom. Valley fold the bottom point at the side points. Unfold.

5

Mountain fold the right point to the left point.

Make an inside **reverse** fold on the middle crease (see page 8). As you do this, pinch the point. It should stick out of the inside reverse fold. This forms the tail.

7

Valley fold the right point halfway to the new crease. Unfold.

6

Rotate the model so the center fold is at the top. Valley fold the right point to the vertical **crease**. Unfold.

9

Valley fold the left point. Make an outside reverse fold to form the ears (see page 9).

10

Cut the ears apart along the center crease.

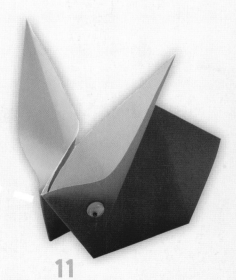

11

Gently pull the ears open. Glue a googly eye to each side of the head.

CUTE CAT FACE

- paper (square)
- marker
- googly eyes
- glue

1

Place the paper on the table with one point at the top. Your cat will be the color of the facedown side.

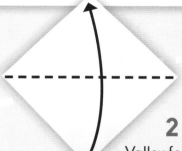

2

Valley fold the bottom point to the top point.

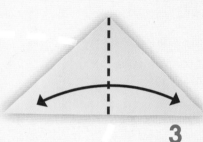

3

Valley fold the right point to the left point. Unfold.

4

Valley fold the left point. The point should stick up above the side.

5

Valley fold the right point the same way.

6

Valley fold the
center point.

7

Valley fold
the bottom
edge.

8

Turn the model
over from side
to side.

9

Draw on a nose
and **whiskers**.

10

Glue on the
googly eyes.

GREAT GOLDFISH

- paper (square)
- scissors
- googly eyes
- glue

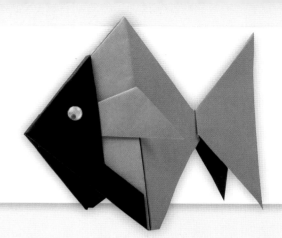

1

Place the paper on the table with one point at the top. Your fish will be the color of the facedown side.

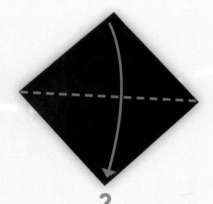

2

Valley fold the top point to the bottom point.

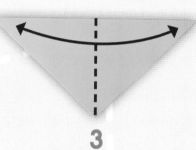

3

Valley fold the right point to the left point. Unfold.

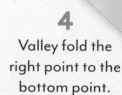

4

Valley fold the right point to the bottom point.

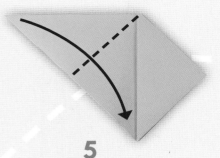

5

Valley fold the
left point to the
bottom point.
Now you have
a square.

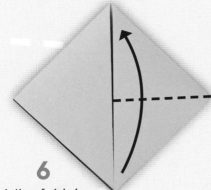

6

Valley fold the
top layer of the
right half up to
the top point.

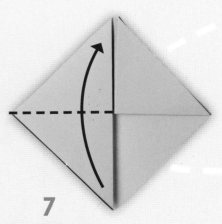

7

Repeat with
the left half.

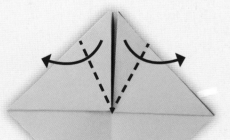

8

Valley fold the
halves of the top
point so they stick
out on each side.

Continued
on the
next page.

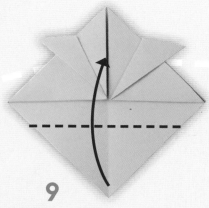

9

Valley fold the top layer
of the bottom point
almost to the top point.

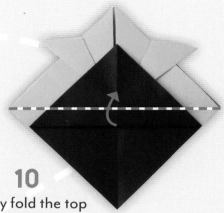

10

Valley fold the top
layer up on the center
crease. This creates
a narrow strip across
the model.

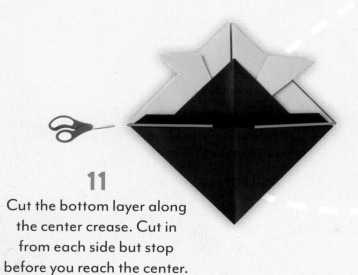

11

Cut the bottom layer along
the center crease. Cut in
from each side but stop
before you reach the center.

12

Mountain fold the bottom
point to the top point.

13

Lift the top layer of the
bottom edge. Push the
side points together.
Press the model flat.

14

Fold the tail back into
an outside **reverse**
fold (see page 9).

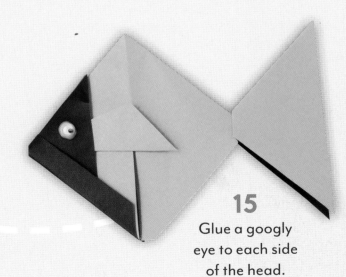

15

Glue a googly
eye to each side
of the head.

PERKY
PUPPY

- paper (square)
- googly eyes
- glue

1

Place the paper on the table with one point at the top. Your puppy will be the color of the facedown side.

2

Valley fold the right point to the left point. Unfold.

3

Valley fold the two side points to the center **crease**.

4

Turn the model over from top to bottom.

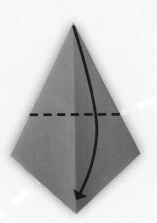

5

Valley fold the
top point to the
bottom point.

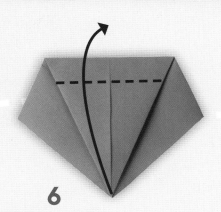

6

Valley fold the point
back up so the fold is
just below the top edge.

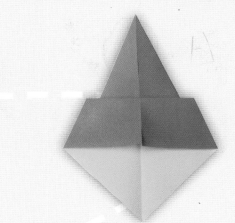

7

Turn the model over
from side to side.

8

Valley fold the bottom
point up to where the
flaps meet.

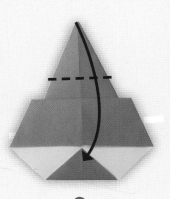

9

Valley fold the top point
down slightly below
where the flaps meet.

Continued
on the
next page.

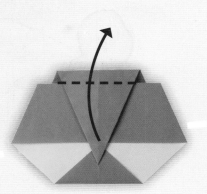

10

Valley fold the same point back up so the fold is just below the top edge.

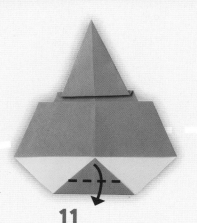

11

Valley fold the lower point down so it sticks out below the bottom edge.

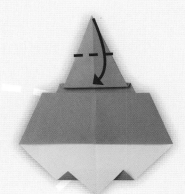

12

Valley fold the top point down to the first fold.

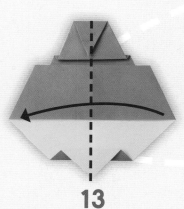

13

Valley fold the right point to the left point.

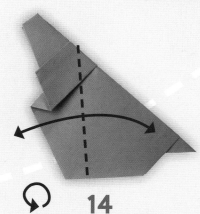

14

Rotate the model to the left. The short open side should be at the bottom. Valley fold the right side to the left so it sticks out past the side. Unfold.

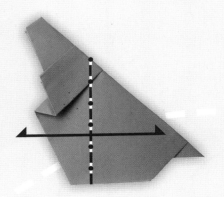

15

Mountain fold on the same **crease**. Unfold.

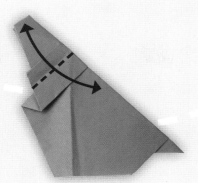

16

Valley fold the top just below the first fold. Unfold.

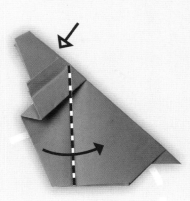

17

Push on the top of the center fold. Separate the layers on the left side. Fold them back on each side at the vertical crease.

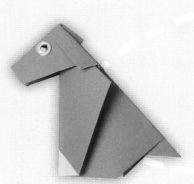

18

Glue a googly eye to each side of the head.

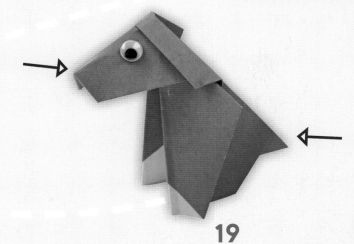

19

Gently push the nose and tail toward each other. Now your dog can sit!

LEAPING
FROG

- paper (square)
- googly eyes
- glue

1

Place the paper on the table with a straight edge at the top. Your frog will be the color of the facedown side.

2

Valley fold the right side to the left side.

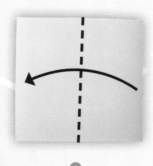

3

Valley fold the upper right point to the left side. Unfold.

4

Valley fold the upper left point to the right side. Unfold.

5

Mountain fold the top edge where the two **creases** cross. Unfold.

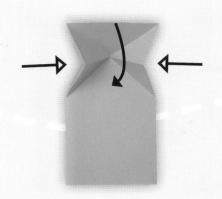

6

Push the sides toward the center. Fold the top down to form a triangle at the top.

7

Valley fold the top layer of the right point. The point should stick out a little.

8

Valley fold top layer of the left point the same way.

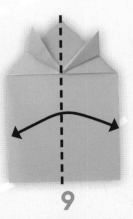

9

Valley fold the right side to the left side. Unfold.

Continued on the next page.

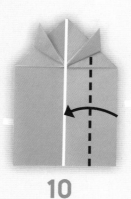

10

Valley fold the right side
to the center **crease**. Tuck
it under the right point.

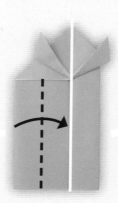

11

Valley fold the left side to
the center crease. Tuck it
under the left point.

12

Valley fold the
bottom corners
to the center.
Unfold.

13

Valley fold the bottom
edge to where the top
corners meet. Unfold.

14

Unfold both sides.

15

Mountain fold both
bottom corners to the
center crease. Unfold.

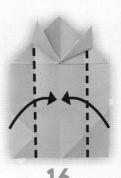

16

Valley fold the sides in again.

17

Pull the top layer of the bottom corners up and away from the center. Valley fold the bottom edge up to the second **crease**.

18

Valley fold the top point to the bottom edge.

19

Turn the model over from side to side. Valley fold the top layer of the bottom edge. It should stick up above the top edge.

20

Turn the model over from top to bottom. Glue on the googly eyes. Tap the fold on the top of the frog's back to make it jump!

TERRIFIC TURTLE

- paper (square)
- scissors
- googly eyes
- glue

1

Place the paper on the table with one point at the top. Your turtle will be the color of the facedown side.

2

Valley fold the bottom point to the top point.

3

Valley fold the right point to the top point.

4

Valley fold the left point to the top point. Now you have a square.

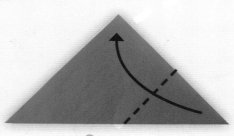
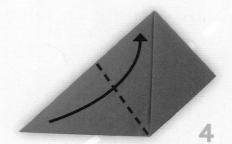

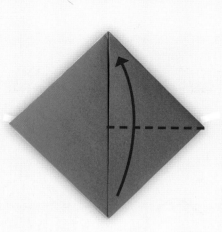

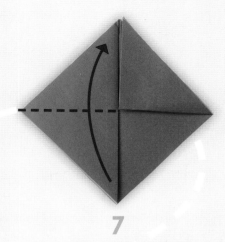

5

Rotate the model so the open point is at the bottom.

6

Valley fold the top layer of the right point to the top point.

7

Valley fold the top layer of the left point to the top point.

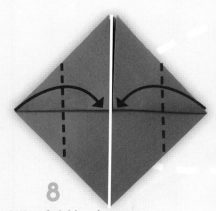

8

Valley fold both side points to the center **crease**.

9

Valley fold the top layer of the top right point along the right fold. The point should stick out a little.

Continued on the next page.

10

Valley fold the top layer of the top left point along the left fold.

11

Valley fold the right side to the left side. Unfold.

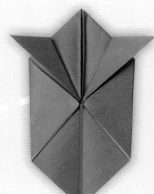

12

Cut the top layer of the bottom point along the center **crease**. Stop cutting where the points meet in the center.

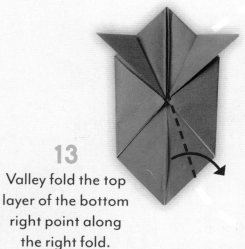

13

Valley fold the top layer of the bottom right point along the right fold.

14

Valley fold the top layer of the bottom left point along the left fold.

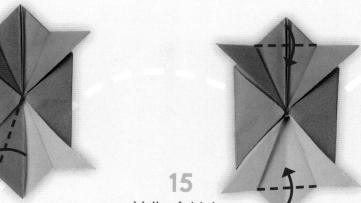

15

Valley fold the top and bottom points to form straight edges.

16

Valley fold the top point up so the fold is just below the top edge. This forms the turtle's head.

17

Valley fold the bottom point down so the fold is just above the bottom edge. This forms the tail.

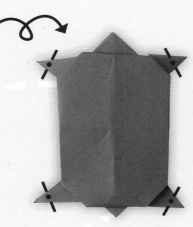

18

Turn the model over from side to side. Mountain fold the tips of the four points. These are the legs.

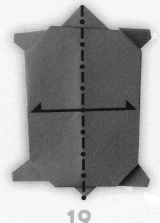

19

Mountain fold the right side to the left side. Unfold.

20

Glue on the googly eyes.

GLOSSARY

accurate — exact or correct.

amaze — to surprise or fill with wonder.

crease — 1. a line made by folding something.
2. to make a sharp line in something by folding it.

diagram — a drawing that shows how something works or how parts go together.

optional — something you can choose, but is not required.

reverse — backwards, in the opposite direction.

symbol — an object or picture that stands for or represents something.

whisker — one of the long hairs around the mouth of an animal.